SAVING A SOUL

Compiled by

Hareem Fatima

Saving A Soul | **Hareem Fatima**

Saving A Soul | **Hareem Fatima**

Woven Words Publishers OPC Pvt. Ltd.

Registered Office:

Vill: Raipur, P.O: Raipur Paschimbar,

Dist: Purba Midnapore,

Pin: 721401,

West Bengal, India.

Branch Office (Operations): Hyderabad

www.wovenwordspublishers.com

Email: publish@wovenwordspublishers.com

First published by Woven Words Publishers OPC Pvt. Ltd., 2018

Copyright © Hareem Fatima, 2018

POETRY

IMPRINT: WOVEN WORDS FIRE

ISBN 13: 978-93-86897-45-9
ISBN 10: 93-86897-45-8

Price: $ 25/₹ 350

Printed and bound in India by Woven Words Publishers.
Printed and bound in the US by Amazon.

Saving A Soul | **Hareem Fatima**

Contents

Eram Siddiqui 141

Ateefah Sana - Ur - Rab

Saving A Soul | **Hareem Fatima**

Hareem Fatima

Hareem is an educationist, psychology student, marketing
strategist, poet and a social activist.

"I am not one of the best poets. I am simply grateful to be one."

*"I hope to see the other contributors spread their wings through
this anthology."*

Saving A Soul

Forgive me if I speak these words
But they are pure and true.
The heart aches when these bonds break,
But I cannot do much to help you.

So why don't you try to force a smile?
It might not be that hard.
Faking it may bother you a while;
But it's better than remaining scarred.

I ask for a favour—
To remain strong and brave.
Like a flower that disallows itself to wither.
Yes, it's your soul I need you to save

Forgive me if I have spoken too much
But this is what I need you to do
Be a diamond which will never rust
I need you. To save you.

Scissors And Butterfly Wings
(Inspired by Maya Angelou)

Does my haughtiness upset you?

Like the sun and moon is mine

Does my resilience offend you?

And my silly twisted rhymes?

Do you want me to become dirt?

So you can bury my spirits beneath?

And how I choose not to be a body of stone?

Does it bother you that I still feel and speak?

Have you not sharpened your tools today?

Your scissors; your fluffy deceit, your lies?

Have you not injured me enough?

Do you still not understand?

That I will rise!

Saving A Soul | **Hareem Fatima**

I will rise, I will soar, I will fly
I will moan, I will weep, I will sigh
I will laugh, I will smile, I will try
My wings will never be cut.
My spirits will never die.

I will be kicked, I will be shoved,
I will be kissed, I will be loved
I will live before I die.
Whatever happens, I will still fly.

Up from above
The heavens shall cast down gentle snow.
To cool my brows after each escapade
This lantern of light I hold shall never fade.

Up from above
While I'm soaring in the skies.
I will be given warm sunlight
To melt my frozen soul
To remind me to never forget my goal

Saving A Soul | **Hareem Fatima**

I must continue to rise.
And now that it is night,
Another battle has been fought
My wings drop me off at Jupiter
To let my mind cool off
In the serenity of nothingness.

Times like this,
When I lay my armour down,
I ask myself and the glittery stars above
"Will I be missed?"
"Will I be loved?"
I wear my tears as a necklace and as a crown
Because in this life, this is all I have
Everything upside down.

I'm Sorry But This Is Life

I'm sorry; please listen
To what these tears have to say.
The words are stuck in my throat
But I guess I have to force them out today.

You can only see this radiant smile
But I'm completely damaged from within.
My own emotions have devoured my heart
Yet I am still connected to you.
I'm finally saying all this, so please believe it
This warmth that you feel from me.
I've created it artificially. Just for you

I hope you can surrender to your emotions
And yet be at peace at the same time.
Just look at how we live under the same moon
Trust that I'll be back to you soon

Saving A Soul | **Hareem Fatima**

It's soothing knowing that we live under the same sky.

But when it rains on me, I know it rains on you too.

I wish I could hug you

But I have so much to do.

So much to prove

Just wait for me, I'll be back soon.

I have to work hard

And make sure this light in me

Shines so bright.

That it can reach you all

Heal you all, teach you all

Inspire you all.

I need to show you what rising feels like

After every devastating fall.

You ask me why I'm like this

You wonder why I don't talk much to you.

I'm sorry. My heart is dead.

What else can I do?

19

Saving A Soul | **Hareem Fatima**

I'm so used to this silence
That your kindness feels like chains
That will bind me to the ground
And make me weak once again.

I am sorry but this is life—
A microscopic part of it...
All I ask of you
Is to understand me

Be with me.

Love me.

And trust me.

You are my mom, my dad, my friends,
My family, my haters, my supporters,
My enemies and spectators.

Saving A Soul | **Hareem Fatima**

That day will come
When I finally hear those words
"Son, I'm so proud."
And that's when I will take a bow
And thank each one of you
For being a faithful crowd.

Saving A Soul | **Hareem Fatima**

I am Not A Poet

I am not a poet

I am a poem.

For wisdom seekers

To plunge in.

I am not a poet

I am words

That common people

Believe saying aloud is a sin.

I am not a poet

I am a song

Eerie hope

Stretching light-years long.

I am not a poet

I am a riddle

Which requires an answer.

That can be wrong.

Saving A Soul | **Hareem Fatima**

I am not a poet

I am a wish

That grants subtle desires

Served on a water-soaked dish.

I am not a poet

I am a dealer

In exchange for impatient time

I give you tranquillity.

I am a healer.

Volcano

I erupted; I was sad
I let out all the garbled emotions I had.
I cried and then yawned
Then a sudden realization dawned.

What is it all for?
The eruption only sinks my heart more
Drowning in melancholy
I attempt to breathe
One brief moment of patience
Is all I need.

My blood completely spiked with pain
Needs no more than to be diluted of disdain.

Planting trees of love,
Gives birth to more love
And the fruits have seeds
When planted—emerge into flowers of ecstasy

Saving A Soul | **Hareem Fatima**

Eruption of pink, flowery love

Cooled down by hails of serenity

Spreads and flows as delicious wine in my blood

And henceforth,

I allow these newcomers to flood.

The Black Rose

Planted in fields of darkness
Etched with patterns of pain.
The once beautiful rose
Is dying once again.

The rose is dead
And yet it still stands.
To die and be resurrected once more
By the gardener's merciful hands.

The gardener has been kind
Watering it with execration.
Growing it under the sun of heteronomy
Forming a new deadly creation.

The rose existed
And this was its crime.
The colour and light now sucked out
Will now allow them to sleep through time.

Saving A Soul | **Hareem Fatima**

The black still strives for red;

For colour and life.

Know better, you cowering flower

To try no more.

It will be inevitably stolen from you again.

That's for sure.

The Nihilist

Let me cry a river

And burn in the sun

To become ashes

Far away from everyone.

There is a blue sky

That I cannot see

I seem like an ignoramus

But this is me.

In my own world

I have built a castle of love

Where glittery snow

Falls from above.

And cools the flames

Of hatred and fear,

In the men who build no castles

Even when their legacies,

The end is near.

Saving A Soul | **Hareem Fatima**

I am no fool.

But I may seem to be one.

I dream of peace and fiery passion

That lives in the minds,

And the hearts of everyone.

If I seem funny

Let me build a grave

in this castle of mine.

To dream no more

To love none.

Hopes diminished,

strangled and confined.

Madness

Pity.

I pity you.

And I pity me.

The world is

Falling in chaos,

You see.

But I guess that

You already know that

And are clearly

Content with it.

Pity.

I pity you.

And I pity me.

Saving A Soul | **Hareem Fatima**

Mock me and

My verses.

Shroud me in

Disdain and curses.

Mock me and

My simple dream.

For us to move,

Steadily as a

Pebble in a stream.

Life is that simple

Is it not?

Oh, I have forgotten.

How we've become slaves of

Our own distraught!

Our thoughts are garbled!

We don't know what we want.

We want fame

We want love

Saving A Soul | **Hareem Fatima**

Side-by-side

We do not.

The Nihilists are

At war with the liberals.

And conservatives now live in shame.

So much confusion

So much madness.

Aren't we all so simple!

Meat-suits with a name?

What can fill our undying hunger?

Who can give the orphan his rights?

How can we be thankful to the anxious mothers?

Who pray for their child every night!

Before she awakes

By the ringing of her phone.

"Ma'am, we are sorry. But

Saving A Soul | **Hareem Fatima**

your son cannot come home",

Someone says.

She hangs up and cries in despair

And drowns herself in her own dismay.

Her son has been killed!

She is now gasping for air

Until she is free...

Free of this madness

Created by you and me.

She smiles as she tells

The angels.

"I pity no one.

But only me.

The darkness is my heart

Has killed my son

And now it has me."

My Dance Partners: Poetry And Melancholy

Come now, Melancholy

A seductive young man dressed in black

Hold my hand and grab me gently by the waist...

And allow me to fall into a mystical trance

Let us dance in the ballroom

Full of gawking young men and women

Their gaze tearing at us like spears

And why should they not envy our love, dear?

We have been bonded since we were young

Bonded by hearts, bonded by tongue

The melody of approving birds sung

Yet all changed when Poesy intervened...

A gentle young man, dressed in blue

He wanted to come in between me and you

He boldly spoke of your arrogance

He warned me about your self-centeredness

Saving A Soul | **Hareem Fatima**

Oh fair melancholy,

Why were Poesy's words so true?

You had me trapped and fooled

Over my senses and my youth, you unjustly ruled

Now that I am a good age of 21

I claim that my real life has begun

Poesy being my one true love

Has saved me from you O' melancholy

A monster sent from above

I still remember how we danced

How I thought that I had no one else

How unruly of you to make me think that

You never thought about what I felt.

Dancing to gentle music

You used to woo me with clever words

You were all I have and all I would need

Again, I complain that to my heart you gave no heed

Saving A Soul | **Hareem Fatima**

So Poesy came and did the noble deed
Took out his sword and decapitated you so gracefully
There I stared at you lying in a pool, ruby red
Ironically I smiled and rejoiced that you were now dead

Good days were now ahead
For Poesy saved my life

A handsome fellow dressed in blue
Yes, Poesy it is you...

All those gawking men and women
Are at peace at how we did unite
Radiant aura of mighty strength now fills the ballroom
As we both have transformed into a mystical healing light

Our dance heals each other
And heals all the rest in the ballroom
We are now smiling and engulfed
By oh so powerful ecstasy
Fated by the stars as bride and groom

Saving A Soul | **Hareem Fatima**

My dance partners, these two noblemen

One of darkness and one of light

I thank you for making me what I am today

This world's own flower of light...

The Animal called Man

I can't. I can't explain.

The roots of all this despair and disdain

All I have is a name

It is the story,

"The Animal called Man"

He is friendly and vivacious

He likes to create and demolish

He is the master and the pet

He is the star of our little circus

He roars and also shrieks in fear

He is the panther and the deer

He is the cobra, with merciful venom

And yet in his venom, lies the cure

Interesting creature for sure

Saving A Soul | **Hareem Fatima**

The star of our circus
Is tired after another show
He has played his mundane role

And now contemplates which way to go
He could meet up with the other stars
But that would be cruel

As in the show he treated them as mules

But he is a social animal
He must love and cherish
In the meantime,

The beast inside him can perish

He must be the bird who
Provides for his young
And gather beetles and berries
While the morning songs are sung

Saving A Soul | **Hareem Fatima**

How quaint is the man

Who is called an animal

For only trying to survive

Time's up!

That is it for dreams

Go back to work

And make the crowd scream.

Sleep

Silently sleep
And fall mesmerized in
A dark ocean deep
Where all the memories you keep
Come alive in your dreams

Flow gently in the streams
Sailing in a yacht full of cushiony thoughts
Breath slowly now
Amongst bliss, you currently walk

Cherish this shallowness
Of a meaningless realm
Awake you then euphoric and satisfied
As the fluffy dreams still overwhelm
Then awake you,
Ready for another day
For sleeping you still are
While walking through
The sharp sunlight of the day

Saving A Soul | **Hareem Fatima**

For life is nothing but an illusion and a dream

Wake you, well pleased, well worked,

Death is the trophy you may redeem

Empty Void

I wish I'd just disappear

Only the sound of silence I'd hear

In an empty void, I'd be

Only the creations of my Mind would I see

I'd like to be alone, yet alive

Only for myself would I strive

No more emotions would I need to hide

In a state of true serenity would I abide

I would like if my heart would no longer have to break

Nor would I have to do the same

I would live for only life's sake

In admitting this, believe me, I have no shame...

So allow me to play these games of make-believe

To give my heart some temporary ease

And O' Listener, you may relate

And cool your mind as well as Man shares a similar fate...

Saving A Soul | **Hareem Fatima**

Leeches
(Speaks for oppression, poverty and all forms of abuse)

Take a knife

And cut slowly my skin

Burn it gently

And let the blood boil within

Beat me to the pulp

And push me down the stairs

Break swiftly each bone

And let me cower in despair

The blood is all you need

To suck and gratify

Your wounded ego

Before you succumb to it

Saving A Soul | **Hareem Fatima**

These leeches feed

The scars are etched all over

Badges of honour and strength I call them

Is it not better to rise again?

When pushed lower?

They are everywhere

In my home

Would have it been better

If I were born alone?

No, for the blood

Is invaluable

Why not make it of use?

Give it away!

To heal the hearts that bleed

And for the poor to feed

And to stitch the souls into form

Those have been distorted by greed

Saving A Soul | **Hareem Fatima**

This is what I need
Leeches to feed off me
To take out of me
All that is impure

So that I can stretch out
My hand to aid the poor
My blood the cure
A peaceful death to give life
A healthy bargain for sure

And after my death
When my tongue can
no longer be of harm to you
And when no pen can assist me
To write these unpretentious rhymes

Let my eyes speak
That are full of the hatred you fed me
The harshness they have seen
The crimes will reveal themselves

Saving A Soul | **Hareem Fatima**

From these eyes; pure, dignified and clean

And after my death

Let my body be devoured

By the other predators;

And the roaches and rodents

To their hunger and distress

My blood yet again shall be the cure

Feed off what is left, my friends

So that I may die a righteous death

To not only die for the leeches

Yes, the leeches,

The blood bonded leeches

Somewhere I Belong

I've been spending my days

Amidst a haze

Surrounded by nothingness

I've been feeling lost

Alone with my thoughts

Feeling complete yet so hopeless

I've cried,

I wanted answers...

Why is life such a mystery?

I tried, I've faced disasters...

And now my old days are history

I've found a world where I belong

Where I can be free, I can be strong

I'm on a path to somewhere I belong

And my soul finally sings its freedom song,

Saving A Soul | **Hareem Fatima**

I'm awake, and I'm alive

All lies, now seem so true

In this world, I shall strive

And accomplish all I can I do

This is where I belong...

This is a place where I belong...

A Cup Of Childhood

I visited my grandmother's
House the other day, It had no doors,
And was all pale, sepia and grey.

In the bosom of isolation,
As no one's come home.
It was laid on clay,
And was built with stones,

It had her name etched on it,
But there was no doorbell,
So, I couldn't ring,
Of sudden came an old woman's voice.
It was the soothing sound, of a lullaby
Which she always sang to me,
The lullaby, my favourite,
Been living in the corners of my,
Memories since 1993,
A voice I never thought would be,
Such a part of me.

Saving A Soul | **Hareem Fatima**

A strange, sinking feeling sat in,
As I gingerly kneeled to place the flowers,
Below at the meticulously carved stone,
"I love you, grandmother"

I murmured.
With tears rolling down to my chin,
Soon again, I'd have another cup of childhood
Here at her house.

My Naughty Pen And Paper

Too much to say

Too little time

Too many words

None perfectly rhyme

Over and over and over

Today, tomorrow and each day

Do these little ones cause mischief

And yet all they want to do is play

With Keats' Grecian Urn in their hands

These naughty fellows reach the dainty old Queen

And listen to all those untold fairytales

Of which she did dream

And if time remains

They visit Sir Phillip Sydney

Another mournful lover

A comrade in disdain

Saving A Soul | **Hareem Fatima**

Muses are enough though

Along with the Fairie Queen

Pieces of wisdom do fools like Spencer

Use to wake us all from these childish dreams

And listening to stories as they pry

These mischief makers

Return to tell me queer tales of how

The patron of virgins, St Agnes did die

And about the road that Mr Frost did not try

And compel me to place flowers at Tichborne's grave

A brave young fellow whose soul his verses did save

Oh how these naughty fellows

Need to be tamed....

Instead, below all the verses they create for me

I most cunningly write down my name...

Ruby Red Crystals

So warm, so pure

Yet frozen solid from the core

Misunderstood am I

And so are my ruby red tears

Yet both are precious

Which only adds more to my fears

My poems are simple

Like you and I

So live without

Fear of being judged

Make mistakes

And grow

The deeper you fall

The more you start to know

Soon it snows

Snowflakes from the sky

They cure

And heal

Saving A Soul | **Hareem Fatima**

Every snowflake brings solace

Just like your tears

Even the sky is allowed to cry

The aftermath of all escapades

Of the warriors and the weak

Is the modest damp earth and grass

Then the grave...

Like Sylvia Plath

So be grateful for your scars, young ones

They have directed you to your respective paths

Belittle not these ruby red crystals

These are all that we commoners truly have

There Is No Prince Charming

There is no Prince Charming

Only flawed individuals

Like you and I

I'm not the prettiest

And you don't own a Palace of gold

Yet what we have

Is something pure

Not a naive story that can be sold

We aren't delusional Romeos and Juliets

We aren't conditional leeches

That suck out the lives of the other

We are individuals that bloom

Gardeners of ourselves

And each other

We are imperfect

And lack sinew

And to be honest...

This is exactly what makes our love true...

Saving A Soul | **Hareem Fatima**

The Haunting

It was a journey
Brief and cruel
Bruised, hollow and afraid was I
Guilt clawed into my back and brain
Never was I myself again

In a gruesome state
I was shoved towards
A light so strong
That my hand was burnt
While shielding my eye
My arm now swinging
Lifeless like a pendulum

I laughed hysterically
Then came the tears
Soon I found myself
Drowning in velvety slumber
I was going asunder...
Atoned for my sins did I

Saving A Soul | **Hareem Fatima**

No longer caged, but free

Free from the haunting realm of my own soul

Saving A Soul | **Hareem Fatima**

Fairy Dust

I cannot quite grasp what this is

The undergrowth of enlightenment

creeping into my soul

Which grows and grows

And feeds on all that I knew

Meticulously diminishing the person once I was

It's all about the stories

That are intertwined with mine

The smile of a child newborn

The voice of the beggar forlorn

The screams of the teenage girl

That no one can hear

The scars on another's body

Her dark tale that cannot be told

As consciousness has been sold

And the man who strives to feed

His empty soul

His existence tied to social norms

And meaningless goals

60

Saving A Soul | **Hareem Fatima**

The animals, insects, landscapes, forests and unsettled sea

The wounded fox, the busy bumble bee

All fixed and directed by nature's scientific mind

The work of a prodigy the world is?

Or something given birth by time?

Am I making any sense to you, O' reader?

O' traveller, O' wisdom seeker?

Have you not studied closely the tales

Of the disabled boy, the blind man

The ignoramus, the bipolar girl

The transgender folk, the ugly barren woman

Are they purposeless?

Or is there a disease in your hearts?

Blindness in your eyes?

Gently rip your realities into shreds

And into a world unknown disappear

The real of your own heart

With the deafening silence

And the cushiony warmth of truth

Where you can smile

Saving A Soul | **Hareem Fatima**

And no one shall mind this soothing

Smile of yours

That heals you and those around

Where live only the serene echoes of wisdom

That magically replaces your eyes

And softens your tired blackened hearts

"Loss is part of this fairytale

And existence merely fairy dust."

I Wish I Were As Strong As You Think I Am

I've been living in darkness

Unaware of what I am

Years of giving ear to mockery and curses

I soon found myself drowning in my own verses

Heteronomy is still there

What has changed is the fact that I no longer care

Changed values, eyes, soul, new pen and heart

Steadily pushed me towards a blissful new start

An introvert that was compelled to write

Talking to white pages every lonely night

With a mask of a creature that you shall never understand

Is currently again attempting to tap into hearts with the power in hand

This story is about evolution, revolution and rebelliousness

It's about dense aura releasing itself from a petite package of blood and

veins

Saving A Soul | **Hareem Fatima**

Illuminating all that is around
Healing every wounded soul found...

Growing from an unknown void within...

It's about transformation
Of tears into anger
And scars into strength
And fear into passion

It's about rewiring the indifferent heart
With surges of empathy
And the mind reprogrammed
Coded with integrity

It's about a commoner...
Soft as a flower petal
And as calm as a settling
Lilly pad resting on the night pond

Saving A Soul | **Hareem Fatima**

Into a creature gruesome and deadly

That can shred out the jugular veins

Of threats to those that you hide so delicately under your wings...

This is a simple poem...

With a simple syntax...

And a simple message...

I wish I were as strong as you think I am...

This Too Shall Pass

Every morning, when I wake up
A cold, tingling sensation touches me
And then those serene voices arrive
And whisper in my ears.

"This too shall pass."

Then I relax my shoulders
And travel back to the past
I count all the scars I got
And see how everything slipped so fast, so very fast
I too used to say

"This too shall pass."

Love, loss, pain, misery,
Regret, guilt, and the lust to achieve ecstasy,
The fears, the tears, and all the spirits that broke,
The scars, the blood and all the other things that have made me choke,

Saving A Soul | **Hareem Fatima**

Today I have locked myself in a prison of pain

And in this new world, there is no rain,

There are hourglasses of memories

And clouds of storms...

But these voices keep on saying to me

" This too shall pass."

"This too shall pass."

"This too shall pass."

These words bind me strongly as my cast,

These whispers in my ears,

These din sensations of hope that tackle my fears,

Shroud me in the depths of pleasure and pain,

But alas there is no more rain

My good days have passed

Yes, they have passed...

Thunder and lighting,

Strong and loud,

I rise above

Saving A Soul | **Hareem Fatima**

And live on the highest cloud
And burn in the rain,
And freeze in the thunder,
Alas, I have gone asunder...

"This too shall not pass, no more,
This shall not pass."

Yes let me bleed,
So do not say those words again,
Let me burn in my hell
And bleed in my sorrow

And then those serene voices arrive
And whisper in my ears

"This too shall pass, my child
This too shall pass.

Saving A Soul | **Hareem Fatima**

Fahad Imran

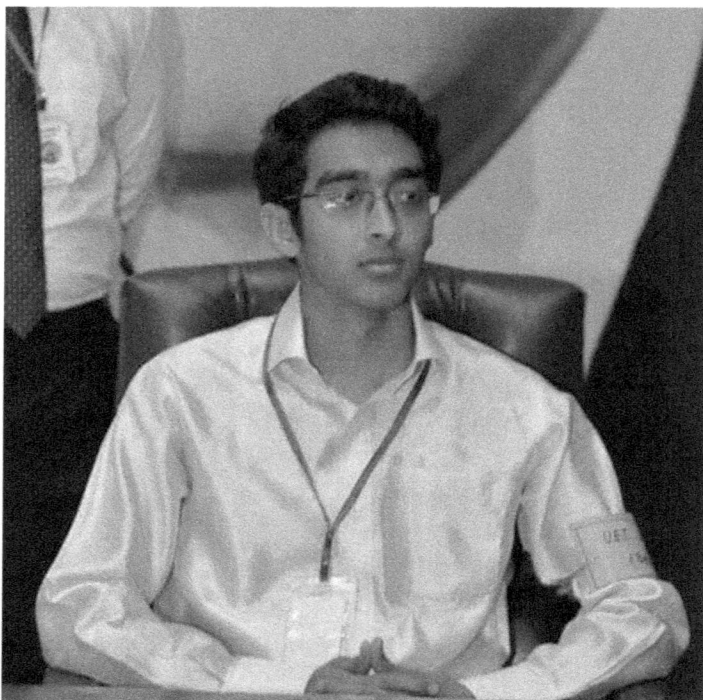

Fahad Imran is another contributor that we are grateful to
have with us.
He is a geological engineering student (UET, Lahore)
but his passion for literature has surpassed even those of
literature majors. He is a part of UET Literary Society

and has taken part in various competitions like 'UAF Literary Festival' and 'The Stories Untold: Season III' held by Dastaan.

He is an editor of the annual and monthly magazines of UET and hence has a good grasp of poetry/article structures. He works as an educationist as well and has collaborated with Hareem Fatima to write an educationist book that shall be released soon. Not to mention one of his articles has been published in Pakistan's first Global Educationist Magazine 'The Reformer'. Fahad's poems are based on insightful, thought-provoking themes each having exquisite structures.

The Discriminant

The men are, to say, utterly cruel,
They give us beautiful flowers,
And they are willing to drown in lakes,
To rescue us from locked towers,

They lay their lives, with care, in our feet,
But we are the sole judge of this feat,
Who needs blood in rags when the riches,
That await us can heal our stitches?

Is my bosom so much admired,
That everyone wants to be tried?
I cannot share my man because of dolls,
Are, sadly, everything but living,

My rights are right to be used anywhere,
But my wrongs are my mistakes, fragility!
Men are easy to manipulate here,
They are mere puppets, stupidity!

Saving A Soul | **Hareem Fatima**

My tear can melt the stone hearts and this,

Is my miracle, which happens thus,

The weapon that can hardly miss,

The target, your faithful, O missus!

Songs are written; poems sung for me,

The sensitive, not so sensible,

I adore those who bow for,

Or submit to my little cripple.

The gender loved most, the prized ones who,

Caused the fall of man, humanity,

We are not responsible! Then who?

The answer is resting in peace, pity!

The False Hope

The contrary of reason,

Is an unexplained diction,

All I do is ask and you,

Put forth another question,

Do I even exist here,

Or am I just a fiction,

I cannot even argue; says-

The empowerment section,

But I can tell you can't yield,

Your train is stalled at the station,

I don't believe in false hope,

"It's just a competition!"

A Little More

Let's go cycling, towards the shore,
Away from far land, to settle the score,

You forgot the times it rained so hard,
The rain that seeped inside your core,

The sand that flies gently through the air,
The time that slips, more and more,

War and peace? How can it be so?
The anarchy composed, the treaty restored,

You say I am not, so be it!
Away you go, outside that door.

All For Your Right

The stars are dark and the sky is bright,
The light is stark with a gloomy sight,

Forget the loon who ran for the kite,
And I stomped on it with all my might,

The jokes you cracked but to my delight,
When I ridiculed and took them light,

I firmly stood to your shoulder height,
With you upside down and me, upright,

It was all for fun, to scare you, right?
Where you cried and did not sleep that night,

Am I the one guilty? Hug me tight,
Will you now, with your lovely wife, fight?

The Sound Of Silence

Have you ever heard,

The cries behind moans,

The way one sulks, thus;

And silently groans?

Bully them as much,

Turn them silent stones;

Take the saved money,

The little he owns,

Show a pistol here,

To a man with cologne,

His child horrified,

There goes his sweet cone,

What have I become?

Why have I not known?

The sound of silence,

In my mind, alone.

The Whisper In The Dark

I heard some noises muffled

And creaks momentarily doubled

Someone was truly troubled

And oh! How his feet shuffled

I saw the drowning eyes

In the salty water that lies

Just in front, with all its ties

To the heart and its emotional demise

Can I help you?

I whisper in the dark

To the figure standing who

On his half facade, had a burn mark

Can I help you?

He whispered with the left might

And I stepped back from myself, amazed

To catch an echo of light

I See Thou Everywhere

I see thou everywhere,

Goes my sight, no matter where

Be it sky or land, somewhere,

I see thou only, I swear,

Voids created, gaps devoured,

Sadness hailed and grins detained,

Thy disgust, for all, showered,

Not, on all, your mirth, unveiled,

Sing and dance and eat and sleep,

Soul desires sometimes to weep,

A thousand secrets buried low,

Hundred mysteries to show,

Cold and warm, thus side by side,

'My love! My goal!' I just cried-

Clouds Clouds Everywhere

Clouds, clouds everywhere
Can I find a sun here?
Rain, rain why doth thou cometh late?
I am sick and tired of your patiently wait

Come seest the time you took so long
Divinity doth do some wrong
Take my tears and mix them well
Should seest someone before the bell

Although the church is far away
But the prayers in my heart will always stay
The passing wind caresses my face
Having utterly misunderstood the case

'Why doth not believe in it my dear
Fear not! Now I am here'
'O wind, o the symbol of the divine
What art thou to give me the wine?

Saving A Soul | **Hareem Fatima**

The wine which I swallowed every time
To live in a happy mood and merry chime
Stray away from the path you do
Art to say me things who you?'

Escapade is violently ill
Shear depression under no one's will
Disappeared the wind in a fraction of moment
Before I could pass another comment

Ye all live in a world so free of care
But get not ye ever the time to spare
Alas, care much but get not so
Expectations are meant to be even low

Aye, thee all have someone to love
But love before confession is a blissful cove
Divinity! Last longer than a man
Lest you give up as soon as you can

Saving A Soul | **Hareem Fatima**

Go away, mind not me

Time will come too for thee

Truth, it might be bitter for thee

Let me say: c'est la vie

Horror O Horror!

I woke up to see my exam to be
Taken up by me; without having tea
And neither coffee could calm this sea
Nor those classes that, I skipped lazily

Horror, O horror! How I wished it was a dream
Horror, O horror! With some topping of cream
Horror, O horror! What to write on this sheet
Horror, O horror! I missed somewhere a beat

My heart stopped beating my insides until
My soul tried cheating on its own sole will
The questions were death; self-pity came in
I looked down on earth and jumped off the hill

Horror, O horror! The blank paper was filled
Horror, O horror! With tears of regret built
Horror, O horror! All those dreams that got killed
Horror, O horror! Man is nothing but silt

Novelty

In the year twenty eighteen,

When I am no longer a teen,

Where kids with mobiles are seen,

And princesses act like queen,

Where T.V. is watched with zeal,

And Satan is there for the deal,

Being hurt and evil is, I feel,

Better than being good for real,

This is the age where we play,

Ludo star, and not ludo; today,

When we used to play with clay,

And wasted in the streets all day,

We lost something in tides of time,

Maybe when we forgot chime-

Of innocence, if it rhymes,

Traded experience with dimes,

Saving A Soul | **Hareem Fatima**

These silicon chips filled devices,

These novelties, these vices,

They give nothing but great crises,

And exchange peace at huge prices.

Addiction

With my new school friends,
I went to different places,

That included a bar,
Where we used to get all drunk,

For days, seven and a half,
Yes, fellows! Seven and a half!

There I saw all kinds of men,
With and without reasons,

But everyone was a hooligan,
Getting excited after a half bottle,

Nevertheless, amongst the worthless,
There was a man, silent of all,

He drank more than anyone,
And was calm unlike others,

Saving A Soul | **Hareem Fatima**

The curiosity carved the question,
And I held it within for days straight seven,

Then, I gave in to curiosity and,
Asked him to spare me some satisfaction,

He smiled and said, "My addiction is not drinking,
I am an addict and that is why I drink."

Dis "appointment"

When you cater,

An ice glass castle,

And the hands that cater,

Your very own existence,

Smash your creation down,

Then, don't worry,

Because of filial expression,

Is an outburst, a rebellion,

Zip your mouth before you think,

Because you stand on their hands,

And they will end your existence,

Instead of letting you down and,

Become better than what you are,

C'est la vie.

Repulse - I

Are you trying to make memories for me?

Are you trying to stop the escalator?

So that I can be stuck at some point and be,

Like you, a society denominator?

Are you trying to make me pose a threat to myself?

Are you solemnly enjoying, being injured?

Are you blindfolding me with passed on lies, huh?

Are you trying to change your mask, isolator?

Are you trying to get a hold, control on me?

Are you trying to be my counsellor?

Are you trying to make fun of me now when,

I know your fake truth, your facade from innard?

Are you piling up a throne for yourself, or,

Are you climbing a ladder to the gallows?

Are you trying to thwart the truth with your lies?

Are you trying to be so hollow, O quack?

Are you trying to fool me or can it be?

That you are fooling yourself perpetually?

Repulse - II

When some things die, whenever they do,

You cannot bring them back; no matter,

No matter whatever you do to who,

You cannot fill the void, the crater,

Again, I am not a third chance fool,

And I am a hell of a traitor,

When I back down from something true,

I become a full-time true hater,

There is no war nor peace, but just hue,

And cry, for the lost calculator,

In the heart, there is no concern left for you,

I am no more your facilitator.

Repulse - III

To all foes and enemies, to all friends and chums,

I stand apart from me, the time finally comes,

After whistling each melody in hymns and hums,

My feelings have gotten far beyond just numb,

Neither am I so great to be prized and crowned,

Nor am I getting pummeled while being sane and sound,

Because unless a reasonable cause is found,

I can stand my ground alone like a proud lone hound,

If I am a rolling stone, I blame no one so,

Let me tell you about my mean skills above pro,

Like a tree-perched eagle pecking on a dead crow,

I can hold my head high and stoop the same side low,

Your hollow facade crumbles before me, I laugh,

Your level reaches not even that of my half,

We work together just like an office staff,

If I am a giant, you're not even a dwarf,

Double-faced you might be so far but look here now,

I ain't kneeling before you nor taking a bow,

I ain't a referee but look, this is a foul,

This is the end so goodbye, adios and ciao.

A Sightless Glance

The path that stood there,

Parting the new and the old,

Saw everything of its share,

In all, hot and cold,

Walking slowly then,

A boy came with a heart to mend,

Who knew from where he began,

And where will he end?

His steps have a beat,

From the songs that melt in his ears,

He stops to see and take a seat,

And watch with no fear,

The green grass fields here,

Wave at all the passersby,

But no one saw that there,

But only that boy,

Saving A Soul | **Hareem Fatima**

The crows flying around,
Fighting for a piece of meat,
Noticed the aura that bound,
Soundless steps like Keat,

His friend that waited,
At the other side, flowing smooth,
His restlessness was sated,
By "The canal of soothe!"

In this age of haste,
Where no one stops and sees around,
That boy with so much time to waste,
He seems saner than sound.

Saving A Soul | **Hareem Fatima**

Anushka Pragya

Anushka Pragya is a poet from Patna, Bihar.

Fascinated by rainbows, she wishes to make lives brighter and more vibrant through poems, finding peace and solace in poetry. She first started writing on the platform called, Wattpad. She has performed at 5 open mics, two of them arranged by YourQuote and Anapestic Minds.

Now, she is known as an expert at writing detailed, emotionally expressive poems.

"Her creation is really good!"

(Zoya Akhtar: Indian film director and screenwriter)

Better Times

Books,

Chocolates,

Nights,

Gorgeous skies.

There could be so many

Reasons to live for,

You just have to choose

Which ones you prefer.

Wanna know what all

Is on my living-for list?

Well, the better times

Make to the top of it.

Don't ask me what comes

In those 'better times'

Maybe just fewer down-hills,

And things looking fine.

97

Saving A Soul | **Hareem Fatima**

It feels like something
Pretty good to wait for,
A notion somewhat vague,
Yet solid altogether.

I believe my heart when it
Says such times will come,
When it'll feel more alive
Instead of weirdly numb.

Times when smiles are
Wider and more often,
Reaching one's eyes,
Making them soften.

Times, when you'd kind of, be
Lesser on the edge,
When you'd not so readily be
Throwing yourself off the ledge.

Saving A Soul | **Hareem Fatima**

Times when you don't
Have to cry yourself to sleep;
When you'd be much calmer,
With a promise of living, to keep.

I don't know exactly when or
What the better times will give,
All I know is that it'll be
A much greater time to live.

To Lifeline

Here's to poems,

Which gave life

To hearts

Forgetting to beat,

And lungs

Forgetting to breathe.

Here's to poems,

Which mixed

Emotions into blood,

And spilt them out

Through pens,

On papers tired

Of being dry for too long.

Here's to poems,

Which untangled

The tongues tied

Uncomfortably in hesitance.

Saving A Soul | **Hareem Fatima**

Here's to poems,

Which smoothed

The creases

On the feelings,

And laminated them

To be kept

Safe forever.

Here's to poems,

Which became

The sharpest knives

To cut through silence.

The strongest hammers

To break walls unwanted.

Here's to poems,

Which helped collect

The tiny pieces

Of shattered hearts,

And tried their best

To glue them together

Saving A Soul | **Hareem Fatima**

Just one more time.
Here's to poems
Which shone
The brightest,
In skies darker
Than darkness.

Here's to poems,
Which soothed,
The burns left behind
By careless words
And actions.

Here's to poems,
Which turned
Into milestones
In the journey
From destruction
To recreation.

Saving A Soul | **Hareem Fatima**

Here's to poems,

Which always

Touched,

Caressed,

Mended

The hearts too weak

To love again,

Too scared

To look up again.

Here's to poems,

Which connected

So many souls.

The injured,

The healing,

The cured.

Ready to embark on

The voyage ahead.

Saving A Soul | **Hareem Fatima**

Here's to poems,

Which became maps

Showing the way

To happiness,

To acceptance,

To life.

Here's to poems.

Ode to Misfits

This is an ode,

A song, a tribute.

To the ones disregarded by the world;

The ones considered stones among the pearls.

To the carefree, wild and the weird;

Or the ones whose opinions are never heard.

To the guy who's always lost in his thoughts;

The one who keeps to himself, feeling he is 'odd'

To the girl who's too much in love with books.

Or the one who's not beautiful in terms of looks.

To the one who keeps falling or dropping things;

The one to whom even his friends never cling.

The one towards whom others are derisive and hoarse,

Just 'cause she keeps writing, verse after verse.

Saving A Soul | **Hareem Fatima**

To the ones always confused or in dilemma;
The ones always quiet, carrying a certain enigma.

To the ones afraid of confronting a crowd;
Or the ones who never speak out loud.

To the ones who're called unworthy and dumb;
After all the bickering, they've now become numb.

To the ones with ideas and views matched by none;
Or the ones constricted by their inner demons.

This is an ode,
A song, a tribute.

To the black sheep, the misfits,
Whom the society forces to quit.

To the fidgety, the awkward ones,
Craving to be accepted by someone.

Saving A Soul | **Hareem Fatima**

Oh, misfits, you don't need to be one of them,
You don't realise now, but you're the genuine gems.

Who cares what they think about you and me?
We can't just let them control us, can we?

So, all the weirdoes, the black sheep, lend me your ears,
Let's go create havoc, without worries, without fears!

Her Silent Friends

She always tried to love her life,
With no option other than to survive.

She tried to never lose her hope,
Even in times, there was no scope.

She tried her best to hide her tears,
Not wanting the world to know about her fears.

She never begged anyone to listen to her,
'Cause she felt, that for others, she didn't matter.

Slowly, she started sinking into herself,
However much in need, she didn't ask for help.

She was getting consumed by her own pain,
All her attempts to speak out were going to vain.

But one fine day, she picked up a paper and a pen,
Which was a turning point, she hadn't realised then.

Saving A Soul | **Hareem Fatima**

The pen started saying what her lips couldn't speak,
Providing the paper, her soul's sneak-peek.

She didn't know but they used to talk about her,
The pen saying thousands of words to the paper.

The solace she wanted to seek in the world outside,
Was never found in humans, even if she tried.

But the pen and paper became her silent friends,
Her broken soul, forever more, they quietly strived to mend.

Saving A Soul | **Hareem Fatima**

Share

Share; share it with us all,
Share; we sure wouldn't let you fall,
Share; make your every feeling count,
Without hesitation, or a doubt.

Share; share all that you have inside,
Share; leaving all other thoughts aside,
Share; we know you can do it now,
Tell everything you want to: why, when and how.

Share; lift the burden off your heart,
Share; your words are a piece of art,
Share; 'cause your tale is worth every second,
To say all you feel, we have always beckoned.

Share; we're not gonna judge you for this,
Share; whether it's about pain or bliss,
Share, we are always ready to hear,
No matter we're away or just as near.

Saving A Soul | **Hareem Fatima**

Share; because it will give you relief,

Share; share your story, long or brief,

Share; for one more time we tell you,

Your every thought and emotion, we value.

Rainbow Of Someone's Cloud

No one's life is ever perfect,
Things are not always correct.

You might think they are content as hell;
But maybe you don't really know them well.

Even if they don't scream or yelp;
It doesn't mean they don't need your help.

At times, they want you to reach out;
Calming their nerves if they ever freak out.

There's no wrong in making them smile a little;
Instead of being harsh, rude and brittle.

Cheer them up when they are feeling sad;
Trust me; it would make you too glad.

The joy of giving is a blessing from Heaven;
Something which isn't received by everyone.

Saving A Soul | **Hareem Fatima**

You are lucky if you got this opportunity;
Of making even one person, cheerful and happy.

If you had the fortune of doing it, be proud;
For you were able to be the rainbow of someone's cloud!

Silence

A million words can sometimes fail;
To decipher feelings, behind the veil.

You can go on with love-filled words;
But still, you'd be near to unheard.

Those words can never soothe a person;
Who's dying under his pain's heavy burden.

That's when silence shows its power;
Making the trust bloom alive like a flower.

Everything unspoken, they start telling you;
But they need your silence for moments, a few.

Your advice or suggestions would mean nothing to them;
If you can't have the patience of listening to them.

You don't know what beauty silence can carry;
Letting free the person from every problem and worry.

Saving A Soul | **Hareem Fatima**

They need you to just quietly lend them an ear;
No matter if you are miles away or sitting just as near.

All you've got to do is, let them know you are there;
Ready to shower them with your love, heed and care.

Grin And Go On

Life is a bitch, whom you need to tame;
You can't let it tarnish you with a single flame.

Things do happen, and they aren't always in your favour;
But, sweet and bitter are only two different flavours.

Your spirits ain't high? Don't worry, it's alright;
But how can you lose hope before giving a tough fight?

Happiness can only be seen by happy eyes;
Fill 'em with negativity, and away the happiness flies.

No one can make you enjoy your life by force;
No one can soften you if you're being rigid and hoarse.

Your past cannot decide how your future will be;
'Cause of bad happenings, don't let your good chances flee.

Even the wrong today, might turn into right tomorrow;
But how will you see it happen, if you've blinded yourself with sorrow?

Saving A Soul | **Hareem Fatima**

I know and completely agree, that it's easier said than done;
But deciding not to make efforts, how far will you run?

Life's always ready to crush you, not wanting you to win;
So show it you're not afraid and be prepared with a confident grin!

You

Trust is something too big to give to someone else;
The one whom you need to trust, within yourself dwells.

Support is nothing you need to depend on anyone for;
Be your own support, and you, for sure, will never fall.

Guidance need not be sought from someone holding you at every step;
Guide yourself to the goal you want, and don't let your feet trip.

Loyalty doesn't demand anyone else to be true to you;
Be loyal to your soul and heart, for genuine people remain so few.

Love is a feeling too deep to survive in this shallow world;
Get whelmed with your own love before the trap of hatred is unfurled.

Admire, adore and armour yourself, don't allow your heart to shatter;
Look up and realise quick, that it's no one but you who matters.

Tomorrow

Speak till your opinions can still be voiced;
Use the words till their strength can still be rejoiced.
For tomorrow may or may not leave you with a choice;
But to powerlessly quieten up amongst all the noise.

Laugh till life still gives you reasons to do so;
Till you still have time, shimmer it all with a bright glow.
For tomorrow may leave you with nothing but sorrow;
Moments of happiness, from life, you might need to borrow.

Enjoy till joy in this world is still alive;
Have fun till in the ocean of dismay you aren't forced to dive.
For tomorrow may not leave you with enough bliss to survive;
Once gone, this merriment may never at all revive.

Live well till life's still worth giving a shot;
Cherish every second, till in your hands, such moments you've got.
For tomorrow may not leave you with enough time to plot.
Just gather all that life can offer, and tie a perpetual knot.

Saving A Soul | **Hareem Fatima**

Demons

My lips don't form coherent words,

Oh! I can't say how I feel.

Even my pen won't speak clearly,

But believe me, it is real.

I sense my inner self-crumbling,

If that makes any sense at all.

I stretch out my hands looking,

For someone who'd prevent my fall.

I wanna rip out my ill thoughts,

Like the sheets of a notebook.

But however hard I try,

My mind won't let 'em off the hook.

I breathe in short gasps,

As if my lungs hate the fresh air.

There's a void I cannot fill,

As if my soul is barely there.

Tell me five times a day, if you will,

That I'm amazingly flawless.

But still, my mind will repeat,

"Oh, this creature's simply hopeless!"

I feel constricted in these walls,

No, not the ones you see.

There are some I've unknowingly created,

Between the world and me.

Hit them with whichever hammer,

You won't be able to break them off.

What's needed is very rare—

A touch so tender and so soft.

There are aches I can't describe,

And fears I can't speak about.

It's hard to trust my life,

I look at everything with a hint of doubt.

Saving A Soul | **Hareem Fatima**

I don't mean that I'm never happy,
Joyous times do often come.
But in a heartbeat, the laughter vanishes,
Making me feel so numb.

Call me an over-thinker,
But I can't switch off my brain.
My trepidation corrodes all good thoughts,
Like some kind of acid rain.

There's enough trouble to be dealt with,
Don't you judge me by your standards.
You'd never know what I go through,
Oh, the fears unseen and sobs unheard.

You'll ask for my anxiety's cause,
And I'm sorry, I don't have one.
But if a building's ruined by a hurricane,
Would you ask the house for an explanation?

Saving A Soul | **Hareem Fatima**

I don't really expect you to understand,

But at least you could try to help.

I'm dying for some assistance,

Even if I don't scream or yelp.

It's alright if I sound gibberish,

I myself don't actually get it.

But I'm trying to fight off my demons,

And I'm definitely not gonna quit!

Alone No More

Sit beside me,

Give me your hand,

Speak your heart out,

I'm listening.

Even when words fail,

Look into my eyes.

Into your troubled soul,

I'm peeking.

Don't cower away,

I'm there with you,

Things from your perspective,

I'm seeing.

Let all fears be seen,

I won't judge you.

To understand your situation,

I'm trying.

Saving A Soul | **Hareem Fatima**

However long it takes,
Even if numerous nights,
To hear it, up all night,
I'm staying.

You're not alone, darling,
A connection, strong as ever,
Between my soul and yours,
I'm establishing.

I won't say, "It'll all be fine,"
For I know it won't be,
But the needed love and support,
I'm giving.

Life seems dark,
I know it does,
So to bright it up for you,
I'm shining.

Saving A Soul | **Hareem Fatima**

You've had enough of pain,

With all the woes and worries,

To soothe you, your heart

I'm caressing.

Don't keep it to yourself anymore,

I'm all eyes and ears for you,

To let you count on me,

I'm dying.

Help Them Live

You say you want them not to die,

But tell me, is it a truth or lie?

You wish they do not kill themselves,

But why don't you ever try to help?

They're strangled in leashes by their minds,

Their worst memories are on rewind,

They're trying to tell you, but all in vain,

'Cause you never attempt to picture the pain.

Oh people, please lend them a helping hand,

Or they'll be ripped apart, strand by strand.

It's not all just in the head, it is real,

They can't explain every pain they feel.

Help them untie the ropes that bind them to hell,

Set them free of the agony which continues to swell.

Take their hands -which clutch their hair- into yours.

Steady them, with love and care- no, not by force.

127

Saving A Soul | **Hareem Fatima**

Let them cry as hard as they want, but please, listen, for once,
To the sobs muffling up the words, they need to pronounce.
Let them speak their hearts out without constraints,
They're shrinking under the torment, it's hard, now, to sustain.

Their lives are turning dark; their sun will set very soon,
For them, beauty's already ceased from stars and the moon.
How'd the souls rest in peace, if they're not at peace on earth,
Where empathy and compassion are facing such a dearth.

Look beyond the smiling lips, to the ones dying to speak,
Look into the deceptive eyes, they'll allow you a sneak peek.
Help them escape, defeat, kill what's holding them captive.
If you want to save them, step up, and help them live.

Just A Little Slow

I'm not sad.

Just a little slow,

Moving slowly towards

Smiles, giggles, laughter,

Leaving-me-gasping

Kind of laughter.

I'm not anxious,

Just a little slow,

Moving slowly towards

Calm, peace, sleep,

Waking-up-refreshed

Kind of sleep.

I'm not tired,

Just a little slow,

Moving slowly towards

Spirit, energy, passion,

Letting-nothing-beat-me

Kind of passion.

129

Saving A Soul | **Hareem Fatima**

I'm not hopeless,

Just a little slow,

Moving slowly towards

Brightness, sunshine, light,

Illuminating-all-dark-corners

Kind of light.

I'm not self-loathing,

Just a little slow,

Moving slowly towards

Acceptance, confidence, love,

Treating-myself-gentler

Kind of love.

I'm not weak,

Just a little slow,

Moving slowly towards

Power, might, strength,

Taking-down-every-monster

Kind of strength.

Saving A Soul | **Hareem Fatima**

I'm not scared,
Just a little slow,
Moving slowly towards
Courage, bravery, confidence,
Believing-I-got-this
Kind of confidence.

I'm not defeated,
Just a little slow,
Moving slowly towards
Victory, wings, flight,
Never-coming-down
Kind of flight.

I'm not done,
Just a little slow,
Moving slowly towards
Life.
Living-livelier-everyday
Kind of life.

Reminders Of Sorrow And Strength

Me?

I've been with her

Since she was seven.

When her steps were tiny,

But courage, ever-expanding.

When her steps were shaky,

But confidence, unmoving.

I have companions too.

There's one who's been with her

Since she was twelve.

When her love for her friends

Made her go to crazy heights.

When her love for her friends

Involved her even in fist-fights.

Saving A Soul | **Hareem Fatima**

There are more of us.
One that's been with her
Since she was fifteen.
When her boldness was enough
To stand firm against bullies.
When her boldness let her
Kick some ass without worries.

There are some amongst us,
With tragic stories to tell.
Stories which have become
Tales of her spirit, fiery as hell.

There's one whom she's had
Since the age of eighteen.
When the disguised hound
Almost killed the fire within her.
When the disguised hound
Was defeated by her valour.

Saving A Soul | **Hareem Fatima**

There's one whom she's had
Since the age of twenty.
When those she loved
Left her heart so bruised.
When those she loved
Left her to heal after being used.

We?
We've been with her through it all.
We've seen her rise after every fall.

We've been there as she untangled
Every troubling knot in life.
We've been with her as she
Struggled to somehow survive.

We've seen her go crashing
Through all the barriers.
We've seen her get over
All her gruesome fears.

Saving A Soul | **Hareem Fatima**

We've witnessed the moments

When sleep didn't even touch her eye-lashes.

We've witnessed the memories,

Which kept coming back in horrible flashes.

We?

We are the scars,

Spread over curves of her body.

We are the scars,

And we refuse to be called ugly.

We are the memoirs

Of all the sorrow and agony she's felt.

We are the memoirs

Of all bad thoughts on which she dwelt.

But,

We are the reminders

Of her strength despite every pain.

We are the reminders

Of how this phoenix rose again.

Saving A Soul | **Hareem Fatima**

We're the scars.

Fading, yet somehow brighter

Than the stars.

We're scars,

And we're beautiful, we know.

We're proud of her,

And it's high time,

She is too.

This Too Shall Pass

This shall pass.

Maybe like a needle

Piercing through your skin;

Or maybe like a feather

Gently tickling.

This shall pass.

Maybe not so soon,

Taking its horrible time;

Or maybe just as

Quick and sublime.

This shall pass.

Maybe leaving scars,

That painfully distort you;

Or maybe just leaving

With no hurdles to thwart you.

Saving A Soul | **Hareem Fatima**

This shall pass.
Maybe haunting you,
Every now and then;
Or maybe vanishing,
Never to show up again.

This shall pass.
Maybe emptying you
Of all hope and happiness;
Or maybe igniting a fire
From the coal-black darkness.

This shall pass.
Maybe, you think it can't.
Maybe, you think it won't.
Maybe, you think it never will.

But. This shall pass.

Maybe right when

It hurts too much.

Maybe right when

You think you're done.

Maybe right when

Nothing feels right.

It will feel right again.

You will rise again.

This too shall pass, my friend.

Saving A Soul | **Hareem Fatima**

Eram Siddiqui

> 66
>
> *And the first showers comes with the kind of sadness which only half loved lovers can feel.*
>
> IRA

"Eram Siddiqui"

Who's enthusiastic, imaginative, loving and short
Loves freedom, equality, melodies and hugs
Who enjoys the dancing drops of water
Tries hard to spread giggles and laughter

Saving A Soul | **Hareem Fatima**

Who seeks happiness in little things
Loves hues and sounds of harmonious spring
Who loves to dance under dew soaked skies
Also, has a weak spot for McDonald's French fries

Who's a flower in autumn like a daisy
Goes through days when her mind is hazy
Who feels lonely and an utter mess
Needs someone to see through her darkness

Who gets treated like a princess
For being the best daughter
Finds eternal bliss
In watching the movies of Harry Potter

She, who loves and feels
Would like to see a cure for cancer, Maldives and a
happy family

Taste Of Poetry

A gathering of ingredients,
Brought together to settle
The frustrated, thwarted mind.

A collection of figures of speech,
All bound together
To convey the theme.

A few exotic thoughts,
Tethered to each other;
All releasing the flavour of joy.

Some clouds of distinguished tastes,
Mixed together on a large fire
To satisfy the demanding taste-buds.

A box of sweet memories,
Lingering in the mind
To sort out a pair of contrasting moods.

Saving A Soul | **Hareem Fatima**

A bottle of touching mist,

Gently floating around,

Completing the emotional scene.

Inner Strength

There are going to be days,
When giving up will seem
So attractive and easy.

But perhaps, no one will be keen.
She was all alone,
All alone was she in the dark.

Then she found a bright light,
Brighter than the spark.
Do not lose the hope in your heart,

Even on the days when success seems far;
Even when all the doors are closed,
Check for the windows that are left ajar.

I may say things you might misunderstand,
I am a human being
And can make a mistake.

145

Saving A Soul | **Hareem Fatima**

But need all strength

To prove I am not fake.

I have gone through good, bad

Heaven and hell.

But I always got up when I fell.

When life rearranges itself

Unexpectedly in front of you,

Hold on to the strength, hope

And love inside you.

Queen

She says, "I was a Queen."

When all the girls wanted

"Their princes to treat them like princesses."

Even Kings feared her;

For, she radiated power,

Not beauty.

She didn't care about her emotions.

She'd indeed conquered herself.

She knew how to enjoy life

At its best.

She was at war

With the stereotypical society.

She was a rebel, a proud

And determined heroine;

Who'd rather die fighting bravely

Saving A Soul | **Hareem Fatima**

Or save herself,

And escape than wait to be rescued.

She's loyal to her nation,

Not society.

Call her, 'pretty' and she'll smack you in the face,

Address her, 'Your Highness'

And she'll give a peck

On your cheek.

Society taught her to be a princess,

But life guided her to be a Queen.

Thus, she conquered 'em.

All those foul creatures who teased her;

Proved to her that she's better than them,

They were jealous of her power.

She isn't any 'Beauty Queen' or 'Queen Bee'

She's a Queen since birth

And she conquered the world.

A Plant's Life

There are many those who wish
That they were a cloud,
A bird or a fish.

But did anyone ever think
What joy might
A plant's life bring?

How does it feel living
In the sunshine and rain?
What it feels is still

An unknown mystery.
Cause very few love to be a plant
Even in history.

Many say it might love to look around,
Though beneath the ground
Its roots are bound.

149

Saving A Soul | **Hareem Fatima**

Is a plant's life boring or fun?
And does it really love the rising sun?
In the past, a plant's life could've been fun.

For, it was surrounded by
Flowers that smell
And streams that run.
There was much space
And the sun warmed its trunk.
But now the situation is different

And the place has shrunk.
Earlier even the air had a sweet smell,
But now even breathing is dangerous
And a living hell.

How can a plant be safe and sound?
When there are enemies all around.
Let us listen to the plant's pleas,

"Help, help and save us please."

Saving A Soul | **Hareem Fatima**

The Best You

We are perfectly imperfect,

And beautiful within.

Because beauty isn't skin deep,

It's deeper than the skin.

We are who we allow ourselves to become.

We get what we give,

We give what we get.

So give it your all

And don't ever give up.

Be the best you!

Be the person you want to be.

Just remember to be yourself,

Not who others want to see.

This day is yours,

It belongs to no one

But you.

Saving A Soul | **Hareem Fatima**

Put one foot in front of the other
And take a step closer;
For making all your dreams come true.

You are perfectly imperfect
And this is okay.
Because no one is flawless,

No one is perfectly made.
You are beautiful within
And your smile reflects.
The love inside your heart.
So, share a grin
And let others see who you are.

Be the best you.
Just be who you are inside,
Be the person,
That makes you happy

And live your best life.

Cleanliness Drive

Oh, how I long

For the morning freshness,

Which makes my mind work

With all the brightness.

But for all the pollution in the air

My cravings are lost in thin air.

This is not fair,

This is not fair.

How I long to take a dip in

Clear waters running,

Which is so very energizing.

But for all the pollution

In the water,

My cravings are all in the crusher.

This is not fair,

This is not fair.

Saving A Soul | **Hareem Fatima**

How I long sometimes
For a peaceful bliss,
Which helps me emerge

From my abyss.
But for the blaring sound,
My cravings are
Nowhere to be found.
This is not fair,
This is not fair.

Let us embark on a cleanliness drive
Which is reflective of a beehive.
Making our country
Neat and tidy,

Displaying our country's
Abundant beauty.
That would be fair,
That would be fair.

Wild Flowers

Wildflowers, wildflowers,
Grow best with the rain shower.
In cool shady covers,

With the wind, it hovers.

Beneath the green covered rocks,
Near hidden spring.
It will be a bleak world,
If the flowers won't be able to

Grow green on our earth.
I will protect the innocent flower,
O, Lord!

I will pause in my walk
And step aside,
Rather than crush a
Dancing daisy
In the grass.

Life

Life is a drama,
Whose script you have to write
To make your future
Dark or bright
By turning on the stage light.

Life is a cycle,
Whose pedals you got to operate
And you are the one who chooses
To be mere or great.

Life is a giant wheel,
With ups and downs.
Where some get failures,
Some win crowns.

Life is a water wheel,
That goes round and round.
You have to be brave enough,
Otherwise, you may drown.

Saving A Soul | **Hareem Fatima**

Life is a tree,
With branches sad and happy.
On which gently perches,
The bird called me.

Life is a race,
With problems to face
With a smiling face
Cause victory you have to chase.

Stardust

In the ocean of moonlight,
The stars spread the starlight.
On the trees, it sprinkles stardust
And there blows a calm gust.

But on the day it fades away;
Oh stardust, don't run away.
In the sunlight, you hide

But when the darkness rides,
You come again.
This enchanting sight,

Will heal all pain
And bring sweet dreams
To your beautiful nights.

Oh, my! Oh, my!
Stardust, don't fade away;
Stardust, don't run away.

Evening

And there came a moment,

The sky turned grey.

The day, which had been

Bitter and chill,

Grew soft and still.

Quietly,

From some blossoming tree,

Millions of petals

Cool and white;

Drifted and blew,

Lifted and flew,

Fell with the falling night

In the sea of starlight.

Melodies

We are musical notes,

Drifting as waves

Through the air.

Each of us has a unique rhythm;

A different beat.

We are nothing more than melodies,

Penetrating the ears

Of those we love,

And your melody is beautiful.

It moves me across the floor,

As I dance.

Spinning and pirouetting,

Through voids of happiness.

Your breathing is the voice of bluebird,

Your heart is the gentle beating of drums,

Saving A Soul | **Hareem Fatima**

Your ribs the strings of a guitar

And your eyes willful composers.

You're the melodious song,

I can't stop singing.

Night Sky

Some people are like stars,
So close yet so far away.
Some people are like the moon,
Shining so bright, but rarely noticed.

Some people are like comets,
They burn so brightly and fast
That they don't last.

Some people are like constellations,
They look so put together
When really everything's far from them.

Some people are like the night sky,
They look so dark far away
But are really filled with light.

Inked Soul

Don't be scared to write in ink.

Bleed your thoughts,

Let it carelessly infuse between

The spaces of blank paper.

Words

Blood doesn't mean anything anymore to me.

I wish black and blue ink

Would drip from

Every wound of mine

And pool together

To create

A Tangle

Of

Pain,

Pleasure,

Purpose

And make poems

Out of words

That mean nothing

To anyone

But myself.

Resplendency

The mountains raise their heads to look up at the sky,

Looking to kiss the eternity.

Probing for the demulcent caress of hazy clouds,

To solace the turmoil, it went through.

First dribs of rain inundated the rugged surface,

The sequestered waterfall cascades down and embellishes the hilly terrains.

Covering it with the soft, velvety green blanket,

Enthusing life into the once lifeless rocks.

Once among the detritus,

The mountains have found their place of resplendency.

Silence

If silence is golden,

What is the noise?

If silence is golden,

What is a whisper?

If silence is golden,

Why don't we treasure it more?

Twilight

The mystic view,

The bewitching sight.

Oh how I wish,

To see this scene all night.

Everything becomes dark,

The sky becomes orange.

The birds know it's time

To return to their nest,

This is the sky at its best.

People return from work,

And the evening creatures lurk.

Everyone goes to sleep,

I wish to catch this scene

And keep it in a box;

So that it doesn't go away.

Saving A Soul | **Hareem Fatima**

The boon of nature,

Cannot be fully expressed

In literature.

Mommy's Girl

To all those who think

Angels don't exist,

There is one with us,

Always in our midst.

She might not have wings,

Nor a ring above her head.

Her appearance might vastly differ,

As to whatever you might have read.

She brushed my teeth

And dressed me well.

With touch, so heavenly tender.

She tied my hair in tiny braids,

For as long as I can remember.

She showed me the twists and turns of this,

Uniquely mystical world.

She taught me that

Not every cloud has its silver line.

Saving A Soul | **Hareem Fatima**

She held my hand
And guided me
All along the way.

She taught me to find an excuse to smile,
Each and every single day.
She celebrated my victories,
With a joyous heart

And made my smile grow wider.
She consoled my heart,
When it was filled with sorrow.

This angel is the one,
Who made me smile
Even when I cried.

She helped me reach my
Goals and dreams,
And taught me how to soar.

Saving A Soul | **Hareem Fatima**

She made me believe in myself
And taught me to be true.
She taught me to be kind
In every single thing, I do.
She fixed my broken heart,
At the times when
It had been shattered.

She stood by me,
Through all my trials
Even if they didn't matter.
She sacrificed half her life for me
And continues to do the same.
You might know her very well by now,
'Mother' is her name.
I owe her my life
And so does everybody
In this whole wide world.
I feel extremely proud to say that
I am my mommy's girl.

Saving A Soul | **Hareem Fatima**

Fahad Hussain

Fahad Hussain, completed his Hons degree in English literature from UMT, Lahore Pakistan.

He has won 13 National awards for his poetry from different universities of Pakistan. His love for literature will keep on brimming along with his poetry.

He was given a title on the behalf of his department 'The first ever poet of ICCS' (Institute of communication and cultural studies) UMT.

Loveliest O Fair Love

Cupids came and did whisper the claim
Tackle this love and do not blame

This love is born between you and me
How sweet, strange and uncanny to thee

Addictive than alcohol became my heart's call
Forget the past and sway in the romantic ball

I fell for you like the morning dew
You brought in my life a fragrance new

Not word-bound but out-loud silently
Calmly and quietly confess my love to thee

O holy Muse prepare my perfect suit
Guard my way in this lovely pursuit

I feel it, feel it when my heart skips a beat
The crowd seems empty and no one's to meet

Saving A Soul | **Hareem Fatima**

Let's build our house with the blooming rejoice
If thou be mine and I shall be thou voice

Dazzle with me like the relentless sea
Come before, before the claim dies in me

The Moment I Close My Eyes

You know what happens

The moment I close my eyes

A gentle figure touches my lashes

Caresses them

And says, steal her before the sun rays penetrate and dance over her lips

Steal her before anyone else could catch her glimpse

Hide her before anyone else could touch

Because your heart loves her much

Come Hither

Come hither, singing with this rain
On the clouds dancing in their train

Delve into my soul through my tiny pores
Awake me and fill my empty stores

I smell the mist from thy breath
Make it eternal and delay my death

What Democracy?

I feel so useless

Of the senses

Revealing the truth

As two eyes, two arms and two legs

So that both wolves can have an equal share

Am I the only piece left out of peace?

I am being stretched! Not I a rubber!

What democracy? What ideology?

Raped till the death!

I have become a mathematical derivation

Mathematicians are erasing me perpetually

When will I be solved? Would I ever be?

Bricks And Sand Grains

These bricks and sand grains
Tell the stories when it rains

The brick on the top of the building
Says, you're safe under my shielding

But the brick in the deep foundation
Says, if I shake, gone is your sensation

Sand grains are small and light
Would be good for an ant's bite

Make a connection like a body and a soul
With bricks, to build a strong wall
But this mortuary earth can kill them all
The damsel, dandler and the dauntless wall

179

I Want To Tell You Something

I want to tell you something, but don't want you to listen
For the reasons I have, will disclose your treason

When I look into the past, I recall each mask
To frame others, was your favourite celebrated task

We had it, just like the sky has stars and moon
Then stars started falling with the blow of loom

I know- the roars of the river and cold make me shiver
With a shadow, I argue which ends up in a peaceful quiver

Your actions and discourse paint your picture
You'll be portrayed in the pieces of my literature

Next time when you pass by, be particular about your words
Each gesture of yours would be teaching so much to nerds

Dancing Souls

To our dancing souls
Whilst visiting the snowy walls

To the music which narcotizes
Giving a serotinal surprise

To the musician in the Elysium
Plays in the nimbus of museum

To the clouds that hinder no more
Harbinger the septenary lore

To the muse who gravid the song
Will have the hearts to last long

If

If tulips be redder than her lips

If night be blacker than her hair

If pearls be whiter than her eyes

If music be melodious than her voice

If rain be subtler than her touch

If wind be refreshing than her breath

If beauty be thine then she is wine

Should I Be The Words For Each?

Should I be the words for each?
How you feel towards the lyrics
Nibbling on the headphone's wire?

How you feel before going to sleep
Taking on the plans you've made together?

How you feel in the corner of your room
Gazing at the crimson on the wall?

How you feel when it rains
Holding a cup of coffee in your hand?

How you feel when you bump into your phone
Looking at the old conversations you had?

How you feel when you look at the bench
Staunch and lone, empty and worn
Should I be the words for each?

Unspoken Hope

And I waited until the sun drove darkness over me

I rippled like the thrashing sea waves, you did not see

Whilst exiting the beach I turned back to the setting sun

The empty bench and the clock did ask me to run

And I waited until the restaurant had me alone

Lights were out and everybody had gone

The last street where I had to stop

I still had an unspoken hope

Loud And Loud Love

Frost dwells in the dark wells
On the shelve, she smashed the shells

Comes close counts the cells
Two tortured twice he tells

Loud and loud love did shroud
Prick the pound to feel proud

Faint flare flown to fire
White witchweeds the wire

Hermit heads out of the halo
Hail hail hides and treads slow

Accustomed

If only heart was accustomed to the
Language of mind and mind to heart's

If only moon was accustomed to the
Light of sun and sun to the moon's

If only fire was accustomed to the
Wrath of water and water to fire's

If only virtue was accustomed to the
Deed of sin and sin to virtue's

If only you were accustomed to the
Words of mine and I to yours.

When Love Is Sick

Love, when is sick

Needs care with each clock's tick

If not looked after

Could bring disaster

Doctors don't leave their patients alone

Why do you abandon your love and moan

It will die without medication

You'll have to check every station

When it is finally dead

Its soul will haunt your bed

Then you'll regret and the clock will mock

Cruel you, could not even see the doc

So let it haunt you now

Won't accept any bow

So let it ruin your soul

Yes, it was your call

Saving A Soul | **Hareem Fatima**

But you will forget it gradually
Still, you'll pay the visits warmly
You'll have a constant inner conflict
Not as simple as you did predict

Put layers of masks and you will see
Without pesticides, insects will kill the tree

Not Dead But All Numb

Not dead but all numb

That chin rests on the thumb

Eyes wide awake

Tears, not a lake

What craving you have now?

Nothing but another vow

What do you yearn for?

I, there's a lot in store

I heard them mumbling

They want the love of a sibling

I heard them fighting

The want mother's hiding

I saw them drawing

Father's figure whilst crying

I saw them falling

On lover's calling

189

Saving A Soul | **Hareem Fatima**

I felt emptiness

Didn't know the mess

I touched it with a sigh

That hurricane was high

I kept following the beat

With the steaming heat

I had to wash the sin

It plucked each hair from my skin

What sin was that?

I hit the craving's hat

Why do you still crave then?

Because of it; reborn in sleeper's den

Not numb but all dead

Days passed, the lake was red

Demolished O Dear Love

My tears would write for you today
Cruel me, perpetually I made you stay

This love is perplexed, you see
But now I hate the shadowy tree

My sighs will blur with each photo of you
Foolish me that I loved you so true

My Muse! Mercy and end this labyrinth
Only love, except did I demand anything?

I will engrave each memory, each touch of you
The priceless assets now my heart will bore

Not so many but in me, I have one soul
Once dead, will have no call

Not so many but in me, I have one heart
Once stopped, will have no start

Saving A Soul | **Hareem Fatima**

Disgruntled love goodbye to you
Visit me again and I will sue

Goodbye for thou will never have me around
No treads, no letters, no tickles and no sound

Goodbye for thou I've penned my last poem
Heaven knows that it was a lachrymotic storm

O felon cupids, away with your potion
You claim is dead and makes no motion

Yeah So Finally I Gave Up On You

Yeah so finally I gave up on you
My heart and friendship you did screw
I melted like snow melts from the mountains
Didn't know I was cherishing the empty fountains

I thought I lived there near your garden's entrance
But like a beautiful rose without any fragrance
A thought of you made me sway in the bright hue
Look at your eyes, how cruel, gave me no clue

Was I there ever, maybe once or twice?
You could pretend that could suffice
Was I even alive in your conservations?
Everyone, but for me no reservations

I was not, yes, I was not there at all
I removed your last painting from my wall
I abandoned you in my dreams too
The heart beats for one, not for two

Saving A Soul | **Hareem Fatima**

Hey sweet vicious princess, hear me speak

You have a beautiful heart still so weak

And yes, this rose will have no drop of the dew

Because I have finally given up on you!

Saving A Soul | **Hareem Fatima**

Rehmat Tanzila

Tanzila Rehmat is a graduate of BS (Hons) English Literature and Linguistics. Writing is her biggest passion and she loves writing beyond everything. She started writing a year before and has observed herself improve with every passing day.

Poetry is the calling that invites her to step into the shoes of the characters of her writings and firm up her relationship with them.

She is a Golden Badge writer at Booksie Publishing website with currently 14 thousand readers reading her work. She is struggling to be among great poets one day.

Where Are You, My Muse?

Left me unfocused; my muse has absconded
Were not we heartily, mindly, strongly bonded?
Shunned and ignored; so antipathetic he turned
All the grim poetry has with its pages burned!
Made me go blind; my muse turned so wild
Forgotten the art the tactic of how he beguiled!
Perfect rhymes, charismatic vocabulary; all is gone
Never will he come; never as comes the dawn!
Abandoned the relation; my muse outcast me
I miss those days; how approachable were we!
Late nights he could whisper in my ear
The melody, the themes could never rip and tear!
Surrendered so soon; my muse went silently
My emotions and feelings are in collision violently!
The mind is blank and heart seems inconsolable
Even if I won't tell it is obviously palpable!
Exhausted; my muse quietened and shushed
Failed to recall, how to writing it pushed!
No cup of love, thus no drink of imagination
Gone is he; adrift I am; lost is that fascination!

Saving A Soul | **Hareem Fatima**

Come! Where are you my muse?

No! I won't listen to any excuse.

Lyrics are coming by, running in my head

Make me take a pen and wake up the dead!

Love me again the way you used to,

Do not we share the bond so true?

Take me wherever you want; in light or in gloom

Take me to the place where roses bloom!

Scribble across my soul, my skin, my mind, my heart

I don't want to lose my muse that is my part!

Dawn

It is dawn though looks like dusk

Has filled the jasmine with a musk

Come! Let us fuse into the serenity

Come and dance our ways to eternity!

Seems like dawn has dawned on the earth

Let's see how it celebrates its birth!

Did you notice the sky's necklace being taken off?

Or reckon there's no wink and no cough?

Come! Let us think the matter over

Come and search for the culprit. Hover!

Listen to the victim patiently

For it has lost its pearls suddenly!

Here see the sun that unveiled the shawl of night

Is now filling its folds with diamond bright!

Come! Let us witness this mischievous game

Come and observe it's nothing the same!

Curtains at the top are drawn aside

Clouds are pale and pink as a blushing bride!

Stars have drowned in the flood of fiery beam

Moon has disappeared with a smiley gleam!

Saving A Soul | **Hareem Fatima**

Come! Let us uncover the covered reality

Come and see that sun's sweet brutality!

No moon seems blinking no star throws a wink

No clamour, no clatter, not even a clink!

Dropping the droplets of the dew

Night angels depart with their crew!

Come! Let us bid farewell to the notion of dearth

Come and greet the dawn with warmth and mirth!

Blades of leaves are bathed and wet

As the dew drops licked and left to get them set!

Dear! The dawn has appeared

Cup your hands; erase the thought of being impaired!

Get determined to vanquish at every step

Do not think of the consequence; nail the husk!

Because

It is dawn though looks like dusk!

Summer Rain

The kissing scorch branded gentle marks on my cheeks
Blotted freckles forcefully pierced and tweaked
The roads felt like licked by the fierce tongues of the sky
The waters on the ground gurgled and did sigh!

Joyful, warm and mellifluous like birds humming
Summer rain did not announce its coming
Tearing the shawl we were wrapped in
Tiny little drops showered, tapped and grinned!

Splashes did mean as if composing a romantic song
For summer rain it was all perfect, nothing seemed wrong
Every creature on the earth rejoiced, joined the water
Birds' hum, prayer's call, children's titter and totter!

Brought a song that didn't need the piano or guitar
A warm embrace of mists did leave a turquoise scar
Clouds felt like candy floss scattered all around
Occupying the big blue cosmos and the ground!

Saving A Soul | **Hareem Fatima**

Velvety pecks of the summer rain's breeze wafted in
Bringing the tiny balloons of snow as their kith and kin
Flowers' fragrance felt as if procured from the Deer's
Sweet-smelling and perfumed seemed the whole sphere!

Summer rain signed off as sky roared as a lion in a den
With a silent warning letter of its appearance again
Every evidence of its mild crimes was silently wiped out by the screaming
heat
Water from the floors, freckles from the cheeks and wetness of walls
Could not even argue nor could they beat!

Love At First Sight

I saw you and I felt you at once
The perfume, your fragrance that essence!
Stolen kiss; I made to your name
How could I leave when you divinely came!

I saw you and thought if you would give me your love
I wondered if I was for you perfectly good enough!
Stolen kiss; I made to your eyes
I talked silently; truly without lies!

I saw you and my heart bloomed high
I couldn't catch my breath just stroke a sigh
Stolen kiss; I made to your heart
Wondered how should I approach and start!

I saw you and my feelings got their wings,
I danced to the rhythm as the glass tings!
Stolen kiss; I made to your soul
Imagined you as my destiny as my utmost dole!

Saving A Soul | **Hareem Fatima**

I saw you that day and I love you to this day

I promise you my love will never have a bad say!

Now, like the cheerful cloud, I sing so bright

For you- my love at first sight!

O Dear Love

O Dear Love, have mercy on my poor heart
Why can't I be your first; first to the last?
The void in my soul calls you to do the favour
Let it cherish our proximity, let it savour!

O my Sovereign, your nonchalance slashes my feelings
Why can't you be my gift; a gift of healing?
The wound in my heart would never get cured
Unless you medicate, it's utterly assured!

O Dear Love, be gentle with this weak patient of yours
Welcome me with open arms; to death, I'm too close!
Let me also feel the warmth of your tender embrace
To me, it's the only tranquil and serenest place!

O my entirety, be the air that I breathe to stay alive
I have already felt this worldly aura, more I can't abide!
Come for the leaves are still wet, roses fresh and grass is green
Let us move to another world, this one a lot we've seen!

Saving A Soul | **Hareem Fatima**

O Dear Love, do not I possess this right to have your time?
Just a few minutes to be taken to the enticing place and sublime!
My feet are ready, waiting for yours to guide me the road
Let us go to, where we've never in our life strode!

O my Sovereign, be kind to this unfortunate being
I always call your name in any song I sing!
You hold the magnetism that attracts my care
I incline towards you even when you're found nowhere!

O Dear Love, don't be so cruel as it's too aching
You slightly smile and my muse seems waking
I write seeing your beautiful, tempting face
With my heart racing, at the tender slowest pace!

O the Heart of Stone, what if you say you love me too,
My feelings are strong and that they're true!
Alone I am, yes you are not here
All that I've written will be locked in my tears!

Take Me

Take me to the palace of your heart;

Make me your queen;

Do it quietly, let no one intervene!

Inscribe on my skin, leave it divine,

Make me yours; I make you mine!

Come let us go so far, where the winds are seductive;

The grass is green, the flowers are productive!

Hold my hand softly and kiss my lips

Hurry up before the air's heart rips!

Paint the heaven where you and I live

Let me name you my soul; let me give!

Rule over me, make me your kingdom

Conquer the love game, solve this conundrum!

Write me a song, make me your muse

Let emotions be tangible, oh do not refuse!

Wing my soul; hallucinate my heart

Cut my existence from this world part by part!

Fall the night, sing peacefully as doves sing

Let us cherish the proximity; let the glasses ting!

Saving A Soul | **Hareem Fatima**

Sip the drink of ecstasy drop by drop,

Fly from this world of the bottom to the Seventh of the top!

Whisper in my ears the words unsaid

Let us be alive, flare up the fire dead!

Rain like summer rain, blow like winter breeze

Make me still for a moment as waters freeze!

Shine like countless stars together in the sky

I let you cuddle; take me to the world so high!

A single touch of your fingertips on my eyes

Won't let tears fall, but strengthen the ties!

I bow before you and we're so close

My necklace twinkles; in my hand, the ring glows!

Such royal and loyal love that makes hearts melt

No queen in her life would ever have felt!

Enchanted Night With My Muse

I'm the poetess and you are the poet

Let's just create a spellbinding duet!

You give me your heart and I give you mine

Put on the candles and prepare some wine!

My tempting spell-caster, your seductive lure

Takes me to the sinless ride and oh so pure!

Your chanting chants enchantingly without failing

The boat of my love I fear would gently wreck in sailing!

Hum my humming bee and warn me about stings

Your tune rises and falls prompting the tension in my wings!

Intone, murmur, whisper or speak silently loud

I know you're here; don't veil do not dare cloud!

Eyes are wandering, hands are on the table

Fingers are sketching your face even sitting stable!

Your gaze is scintillating in the dim light of a candle

Falling bit by bit; apologies afore if I fan any scandal!

Saving A Soul | **Hareem Fatima**

Pour that crimson red for the two of us
Oh my sovereign, think no trouble and reflect no fuss!
I can read the fear of losing in your eyes, my entirety
You have my hair as your home darling, for eternity!

Have a sip of a drink from the glass of my soul
Can you feel the serenity cherishing in your throat?
I watch your lips wet; the last drop calling mine
Is your presence more toxic or entrancing power of wine?

You come up, hold my hand and stroke my locks
Oblivious to the fact, the world jealously mocks!
The map of your lips to my lips is just a kiss away
Un- the bar of distances with the necking sway!

My eyes are closing at a snail's pace
There' something in the air I can smell and trace!
It's you and your being there in front, secured in my gaze
I could voyage the world despite this fog and haze!

Saving A Soul | **Hareem Fatima**

Shush! The chord of the guitar in your heart strums
Making my fragile body tear in countless crumbs!
I have had an amazing time with you my muse
Far along I won't argue nor would I to your call refuse!

Let's just wind up all these lyrics before we sink
The travellers passing by would detach us in a blink!
Come again in my dream as it's the only secret place to be
I'm enslaved by your love and crisscrossed in your magic tree!

Under A Spell

I wait for you from dawn to dusk
Come and fill the air with your hypnotizing musk!
Make the place so absorbing that I forget
Everything I do, every word I say and beget!

Come as comes the quake without a news
Shake my earth and inscribe on this skin my muse!
Spread on it your romantic sayings' graffiti
And make it immortal for eternity!

I am silent; I assure my lips are zipped
Rule over me until my existence is torn and ripped!
Gradually and slowly, you're making me fall
I'm enslaved by your invading look and your call!

Come as comes the rain and drench my soul
Drop your mystic undertones and mesmerize the whole!
Slowly but surely I can figure out the love through your breathing
Do not forget it's in your spell that I'm patiently weathering!

Saving A Soul | **Hareem Fatima**

I'm feeling highly dosed with you, the toxic song

Your magical charm has wrapped me up for oh so long!

Wake me up from this very enchanting sleep

Oh, let me to my real world slither and creep!

Am I Insane?

You are here and I let you go

How can it happen? Maybe you know!

The dawn won't break without seeing your face

The night won't fall if my dreams don't trace!

I can never let my mind foresee

Life without you; will never ever be!

Water I don't care; air I don't need

This is my love that you have to heed!

Unexpressed hope mocks me a fool

You never accepted but I have a fear to lose!

No, my heart won't permit; it will never allow

To be shut up and leave you for then or now!

Feeling so empty, feeling so low

You've made me restless and you don't know!

I want to hear you once again

Call me now and relieve this pain!

My silent love screams; oh it screeches piercing cries,

I can't keep it quiet with the pace it picks the rise!

Borrow my heart for a second and let it beat

Sweetly painful cringes would come to meet!

Saving A Soul | **Hareem Fatima**

I wish you could sense I wish you could feel,

How the sore longings in my heart would heal!

Don't take me for granted don't break my heart

My body and soul will get apart!

Try to be quiet for a second try not to say

I will be gone but my feelings will have their way!

They will reach your heart; they will pinch your soul

You'll be agitated; miss the moments' bit and whole!

What is it that you're here but still I miss you

Can never it be called Love - that is true?

So deep is this loneliness, even in a crowd,

Am I insane; or you're so proud?

Monster In Love

A monster in love with you

Can kiss your lips; denounce you too!

Beautiful eyes in love with you

Can talk so magical; break you too!

A monster in love never gets enough

It calculates you; only opts to bluff!

Handsome talk and all that stuff

Can indulge and give you time so tough!

A monster in love cunningly rules

Can make you one of the greatest fools!

Mesmerizing words blast tear pools

Can only vex but never get cools!

Monster in love does truly dare

Can never ever take your care!

Expressed emotions that seem so rare

Can take you to the life unfair!

Saving A Soul | **Hareem Fatima**

Monster in love is in the heart so weak

Can never bring joy and take it to the peak!

A silent lover that exposes to be meek

Can blind you and stop you to seek!

Monster in love with you

Can kiss your eyes; shatter you too!

Beautiful lips in love with you

Can sing so melodious; hypnotize you too!

Saving A Soul | **Hareem Fatima**

Married To The Man I Hated

Stars over sky winked up above the high

Lost in here I woke up with a tear in my eye!

Moist eyes were seen quietly set

Pin-prick pain it bore on a pillow wet!

This time is very tough I don't know

If I can manage and let it go!

His single touch cringes my nerves

As so harsh a trembler it serves!

It is not the face I dreamed of

It was something really sweet and soft!

I could hear the piece of glass shattering in me

Are they my dreams or is that stubborn I in me?

Where is the real I gone, I cried.

I'd compromise! How much I have tried!

Things are not working I'm still at my window

The coffee cup is empty; life has stopped to glow!

My hair is changed I'm no more beautiful

I am different; forced to be dutiful!

I had my ways and he has his own

He can't love me; never as he's shown!

Saving A Soul | **Hareem Fatima**

I'm nothing but a servant at his home
Where I've to work and he to flutter and roam!
When would he open his heart for me and care
Can't he leave me? I get afraid of his cruel stare!
Now the night paints loneliness so straight
Stroke over stroke; painful blotches in the plate!
Wondered and compromised, 'it was fated,'
That I married a man I hated!

Sensing By Senselessness

Write with me; help me out,

I'm stuck with words, please make 'em bout!

Take me to an unknown, strange place,

Where no one can find nor can trace!

Fill my pen with your everlasting ink,

Inscribe if in your stomach butterflies wink!

I will show you the path where we'd head,

You keep on writing; my lap's your bed!

Hey, can you hear the sparrow's singing?

I stroke your hair and my heart is sinking!

The bird on that branch smiles to encounter us too,

Now you can guesstimate how much I love you!

The grass is so green and golden fresh,

Our presence together here heavenly mesh!

Can anyone discern; can they recognize?

How strong our love is, they can never realize!

Saving A Soul | **Hareem Fatima**

You get up; caress my cheek; look into my eyes,
I know you too want to knot unbreakable ties!
Please build in here a shatterproof home,
Where you and I live; now conclude this poem!

The night was same; I had the same dream,
You are buried in my soul; my pen does scream!
The garden that was our little love cage,
There you still lie in my lap with a pen and page!

I call you My Muse; help me write,
You are dead, but my heart does fight!
The day you came, the writer in me was born
And now you're gone; again I feel so weak and worn!
It's time so different so strange and oh this insanity this madness,
I sense you by senselessness.

From Affection To Rejection – Always With You

You seem so sad today, why's that so?

Your face's fallen and the mood is low

May I come to your garden and give you a rose?

I know I'm not like the one who's to you so close!

You seem weary, weary of what I don't know

Your cheeks are drawn and eyes are yellow

May I cup your face and give you a sweet hug?

The one that's gentle, secure and snug!

What is this dejection, I cannot bear

This expression I would never allow you to wear

May I come and lighten up your mood?

I swear it won't stretch nor will it protrude!

Is that a mood swing or you don't want me there?

You know everything; why do I ask, why do I care

So may I offer you my shoulder to tender your head on?

Oh, say yes, where you have gone!

223

Saving A Soul | **Hareem Fatima**

I just hate seeing you cry
It agonizes my earth and even haunts the sky
May I come and wipe your tears, my sweetheart?
I promise I won't ever let us get apart!

Why's this happening, am I responsible, my friend?
I wish I would rather die, my life would end!
May you come and yank this floating breath?
It should stop beating and meet its death!

You went saying I'm not best for you
I understood all, and didn't argue!
Be it this world or countless others, I tell you what's true
From affection to rejection- I'll always be with you...!

Because You Are Blessed

Forget about the black and white skin

No worries for the body, fat or thin

Don't think about the gapped teeth and fret!

You're born to cherish this beautiful existence,

Because you are blessed!

Let yourself be free of intrigues and jealousies

Muse over Keats's unheard melodies

Switch to the serenity, be the tranquillity's guest!

You're born to sightsee the world in you

Because you are blessed!

Feel the music of your life

Fight with whatever it brings the strife

They would certainly grab your collar and put you in the test!

You're born to win on them all

Because you are blessed

Raise your spirits up above the high

Wing your soul and touch the sky

Saving A Soul | **Hareem Fatima**

Cross the horizons of North, South, East and West!
You're born to discover your way
Because you are blessed!

Seek the beauty of nature with all your sensory powers
Smell the fragrance of petals, taste the honey and all that's bitter and sour
Caress the softness; soften the harshness by reaching to its nest!
You're born to relish
Because you are blessed!

Don't be scared if you cannot swim
Just give yourself to the water and let it teach you
No one's touched the base without kicking off the crest!
You're born to conquer yourself
Because you are blessed!

Live for the moment you are in
You've got countless competitions, all to win!
Don't submit yourself to the fears screaming to their best!
You're born to kill them all
Because you are blessed!

Saving A Soul | **Hareem Fatima**

The time you discern yourself and get to know

You'll have the rhythm, you'll have the flow

Sing to yourself in the quietness, the stillness!

You're born to sway within

Because you are blessed!

Saving A Soul | **Hareem Fatima**

Ateefah Sana - Ur - Rab

Ateefah Sana Ur Rab is a published poet and writer from Pakistan, who fairly believes that not weapons but words can make greater changes. Her aim is to spread awareness and wake up the hibernating consciences of her fellow beings.

Most of her writings reflect social issues and problems faced by individuals as well as they bring to light; the bitter truths and harsh realities.

Her poem, 'Destination' was first published in the February 2016 Issue of Radiance Magazine by Fahmedeen Publications. She completed two courses 'Writing for Young Readers' and 'Sharpened Visions: Poetry Workshop' from the well-known platform for online courses namely Coursera. She participated in The Stories Untold Competition — Season 1 held in June 2016 by Daastan Publication and in the Poetry Competition 2017 held by the US - Magazine for the youth, The News International.

In August 2016, Ateefah Sana Ur Rab published her very first poetry book, 'Diary of Fervent Verses' on MeraQissa; a self-publishing platform by Daastan Publication and in January 2017, published her realistic short story 'The Diary of a Sinner' on the same platform.

Her second poetry book, 'Entombed Silence' came out in November 2017, published through Amazon. Another short story of hers, 'Perfect Imperfections' is also available there.

Evergreen

O ye, who dwells in sorrow,

Encircled with the dread of the unknown

Ye heart weeps and seeks some help

But all to ever be in sight

Is the clinging absence of the light!

Ye wander upon thine shrewd beliefs

And the depth of damage unmeasured

While a bunch of comrades; with pride

Adorn the racks with trophies again

Along with those bearing layers of dust

Dawn to dusk; ye struggle alane

Awaiting wind to bless thine sails

Falter not and strike once more

It may appear in vain; this life,

But soon ye'll witness the evergreen sprout!

Perishable

Blisters upon the skin
And some embossed scars
Footprints of the malicious
Or some black and blue stars

Glow under the sun
Never in moonlight
With fears unborn
Clawing out dearth
Yet, wide awake are why
All those demons stillborn

Black, white or grey smiles
Denial had but defused not
An alarm's threatening shrill
Came saviours to rescue though
As virtualization played its part

Saving A Soul | **Hareem Fatima**

Freedom attained at dignity's cost

New souvenirs; to be adorned

Worn out canvas; decorated again

Perished entirely; perishable still.

Hush

Hush---- ye little child
Hush---- and get some sleep
Rid off all the thoughts; coiled
Don't let the demons creep

Forget that ye ever dialled
Thine calls all go unheard
Ye speak but the words absurd
And such complaints are never filed

Lie still and make no sound
Useless, it is to weep
To them, ye are a stupid bird
That loves to hop in rounds

Ye attempt still to escape the hound
One that's there but never found
Inside and out; the peace is spoiled
Scars invisible; travel far and deep

Saving A Soul | **Hareem Fatima**

Hush, hush---- ye little child
Thine calls for help were deaf and blind.

Hither

Hither---- a leaf breaks free again
Happy inauguration of the path to doom
Rejoicing upon such temporary gain
All will but; wither very soon

Shadows bewitching the empty room
Choir of silence under the moon
Hither---- echoes; a wish to rain
Obscured within one melancholic tune
Her saviour; lost in memory's train

Heart's garden; awaits its prune
Survival game; life has become
Deflated lies; the hopeful balloon
Tattered buds; now, never to bloom
Absence of hers; brought ultimate vain

Saving A Soul | **Hareem Fatima**

Bright days are no longer welcome
Departed all; with the mother's soul
Petals so exquisite of the cherry blossom
Dead in her hands; clamour in pain
Yearning for what, now lies in a tomb

Enveloped strongly in the arms of disdain
What's yet to arrive beside her doom?
Unpredictable life presents bouquets; mundane
Decreasing rhythm of one beating drum

Not outside; but this time, in the room
Oh, hither---- breaks a heart again!

Well-Wisher

Art thou ready to take the leap?
Bid farewell to the world so soon
Not a fragment of nightmares shall ye keep
But if gone; ye'll be missed by the moon

Art thou ready to be engulfed by the deep?
Stillness and tranquillity that ye did always seek
Though inside that heart; fear does creep
From there, outside; ye'll never be allowed to peek
Thine eyes wander from grass to the moon;
Helpless and scared as one sacrificial sheep

Art thou content to take the leap,
And destroy the beautiful unhatched cocoon?
Bunch of failures that ye call a 'heap'
Struggles, they are; given up very soon

Saving A Soul | **Hareem Fatima**

There's time still for your success to reap
Ye'll find an ocean; just follow the creek
Shoo away demons pronouncing ye weak
None is achieved by those who whine and weep
To glide out of misery; ye must take the leap

Ye shall be blessed with the victor's crown
Satisfaction and contentment; forever to keep

Do not O' friend; bid farewell very soon
Be a well-wisher of thine; just like the moon.

Shooting Stars

I am well aware of the scars
That you do not show
Wondering if it would
Diminish my love's glow

Even if there are no shooting stars
Let the sky remain infinite black
If happiness lies like an old guitar
In the attic; alongside some unused stack
Encircled by demons; I'll stand with you
For here, I did not come to eventually go

I have no intention to breaks the bars
And fix it all with glitter and snow
You're beautiful just the way you are
Many may not but I believe and know

Saving A Soul | **Hareem Fatima**

Do not pray for an evacuation to Mars

Success isn't determined by the trophy rack

You wish to escape and never come back

Tiresome indeed, are these resurrected scars

But only warriors are bestowed such permanent stars

I heartedly desire to fly with you

Make it through the obstacles' queue

Together; let's fight and continue to grow

On the way; befriending one healing glow.

Take My Hand This Time

Take my hand this time
And we shall part ways
Leave misery in the past;
Mistakes that we have made
These boulders on our shoulders
Let's throw them all away

Suffering that seems to last
Won't stay for several days
The nights are getting colder
Our monsters; in charade
Take my hand this time
Let's be strangers for one day
Celebrate until it lasts
And the lights all go away

If this is how it's going to be
We shall never be afraid
Let's ignite the nasty folders
And blow the remains away

Saving A Soul | **Hareem Fatima**

Take my hand this time
And we shall fly away
Leave regrets in the past
And start our life again!

Ye And I

Ye want to close thine eyes

Take a break from reality

Calm down the turmoil inside

As if it were less than the outer noise

Why do ye abhor what is thine?

Accountable ye are not for actions foreign

Oh, why can't thine resentment subside?

Ye are not who inflicted brutality

Crystal clear are all their lies

Pretentious kindness with dazzling smiles

To gain trust, and; to later backbite

Ah, they never intended to mend broken ties

Ye heart lies as shattered as mine

Mourning in silence; two pairs of e'en

As they stare at nothing in utter despair

Saving A Soul | **Hareem Fatima**

Ye and I, let's close our eyes
Breathe out betrayal in smoky sighs
Unweave the bittersweet memories
Losing them in one path unknown

And someday if we pass through
Familiar mist of greyish white
Let's smile then, ye and I;
No longer chained
To the poisonous hue.

Good Enough

Oh, are ye, never good enough?
Worthless like overused stuff
Do ye stall below average?
The unwanted---- cheap beverage

Oh, are ye, always backstage?
Neglected tantrum of early age
A soundless bird trapped in a cage
Beauty of thine---- never good enough

Nay, there ain't anyone who cares
None want to pay some extra fares
To them, ye are, never good enough
Oblivious of smooth; beneath the rough

But, shall not, ye feel resentment or rage
Never have ye been not good enough
Do not, my friend, shed more tears
Never have ye been below average

Saving A Soul | **Hareem Fatima**

Exquisite are all thine broken layers
To join them; ye have already done enough
Ye might be a book with very old pages
But thine worth has always been there
Trust me, ye are, perfectly good enough.

Alive

Ye harm thyself to feel the pain
For it does but make you feel alive
Till numbness overcomes ye once again

Ye brew no credence in struggle's sails
Oh, it is but all in ultimate vain
Hopes invisible; be it an hour or day five
Ye cannot see; in fighting, no gain
Oh, why is it all in ultimate vain?

Attempts fruitless are all thine strives
Life is like a honey-less beehive
Obstacles and failures sting once again

Ye harming thyself is of no gain
With sorrows that have yet to arrive
Let thyself drench in the soothing rain
And then, may thine inner child feel alive

Saving A Soul | **Hareem Fatima**

From enjoying life, do not refrain

Treat thyself better when bad days arrive

Ye deserve happiness and departure of pain.

Light We Cannot See

All the light we cannot see
Hides what is meant to be
Beyond chains that fall free
Known by the book of eternity
Oh, we shall; with time, understand

We see but the barren tree
Unaware of the obscured reality
All the beauty we cannot see
Oh, we shall; with spring, understand

Life is indeed; one rubber band
Blessed with the gift of elasticity
Oh, we shall; if we ponder, see

It is but, not a shopping spree
Depreciable unluckily; is the living strand
None have escaped their fatality

Saving A Soul | **Hareem Fatima**

Oh, we must; before death, understand
Happiness and sorrow; come hand in hand

All the hopes we cannot see
Reside in the familiar vicinity
Oh, we must; open our hearts to see.

Essence Of Gold

Gone rigid at the touch of cold

Ungranted wishes and hopes denied

Trapped within those bubbles of breath

In vain, clamour upon hitting the surface

Surely, this will end tonight

No more regrets---- never again to hold

Darkness has all along been a friend

Standing by when sunshine betrayed

The sole companion to embrace flaws

Ah, but those demons; were never defied

Skin at mercy of bloodthirsty claws

Decorated with patterns of unhealed scars

Failures on the walls; hanging like a wreath

Body still struggles to reach the surface

Oh, it does not want this life to end

That heart, too, beats despite the flaws

Saving A Soul | **Hareem Fatima**

A wish is there to erase absence of light
No matter if good days have been delayed
Hidden behind clouds are brightest stars

There's a lot in life waiting to unfold
The goodness is like a sword in sheath
To shine; it needs to be taken out

Every story that has ever been told
Has its own depth and essence of gold.

Gone

Gone hath the one ye did trust
Like seeds disappearing into dust
Gone hath the hopeful ray
With the one who did not stay
Memories of thine; the cause of pain
Or some expectations; gone in vain

Deceived and shattered, lies thy heart
Calm before the storm was never seen
True, alas, this moment should've never been

Ye cry each night; usher thyself to sleep
Drenched pillow stays still in silence
While the forlorn moon lets out a sigh
Both pray together when ye are asleep
For happiness to enter that grieving heart

Saving A Soul | **Hareem Fatima**

It is time to wipe away those tears

And to let go of all thine fears

Treat thyself with gummy bears

And gone shall be, the sorrows of today

Brighter mornings await in line

Soon ye'll see and come to love

The calming azure of the sky above

And then, finally the suffering of today

Along with the wind; shall be gone.

Phobia

Etched on white; the crimson map

Familiar face adorning eyes of stone

Predicted return yet not so bright

Eternally chained to the dark fortress

For victims of murder; there is no light

'Oh, don't you remember, my dear mother?

This string of life was cut by you

Officially there may haven't been a case

The truth remains concealed by none but you

Those hands of yours, oh precious mother,

Haven't you washed so many times?

There is not any---- no stain in sight

But you are aware and I know it too

My blood's right there and it points at you.'

Saving A Soul | **Hareem Fatima**

New clothes but of colour; same
Visitors few; be it night or day
Clad with all allegations true
Into nothingness; grey orbs stare
Memories locked in an abandoned train
With a working engine that never stops
A circular railway; going round and again

'Oh, if I could have died instead of you,
Fate would have then granted you more
A life full of liveliness and free of things; sore
Oh, why—why did I ever betray you?
Why have I become a woman so cruel?
I killed my own child; it's nothing but true
Oh, why hadn't I then, died instead of you?'

A prick on arm and very soon indeed
Eyes close for another round of sleep
Ushered carefully back to the room
Familiar sheets go in a tender embrace
And the wheelchair is on guard once again.

Magical Serenade

And in the magical process

Of sewing the glittery shreds

There were thousands of needles

Unwillingly pierced

To rejuvenate the tattered silvery shards

I hadn't ever known that

In order to blossom, I'll have

To rip apart these velvety petals

And let a cosy warm drizzle

Shower the dormant roots once again

Embrace this soul in a melodic lull

The drip-drop farewells of lightweight clouds

That, like enchanted waves, tenderly hush away

Flustered shoals of rainbow seashells; astray

Serenading them all the way back home.

Saving A Soul | **Hareem Fatima**

Saving A Soul | **Hareem Fatima**

www.ingramcontent.com/pod-product-compliance
Lightning Source LLC
Chambersburg PA
CBHW031338040426
42443CB00006B/377